TO

_____

FROM

_____

DATE

_____

A MESSAGE FROM THE ARTIST

Do you ever have negative thoughts? I do. With 70,000 thoughts per day, I'm sure we all do.

As an artist, I'm often left alone with my thoughts, and for me, that's not always a good thing. I have a tendency to overanalyze *everything*. And when I started freelancing, I spent most of my days drawing, which gave my mind plenty of time to wander. Before I knew it, I was caught in my own downward spiral of negative thoughts: overthinking past events and conversations, pondering over what others were thinking of me, and imagining what they might be saying behind my back...this was dragging me down emotionally, and even worse, I was starting to believe some of my own lies that I concocted.

While our brain is an extraordinary organ, we need to keep it on track. The Bible reminds us of things we should focus on and think about: *"whatever is true, noble, right, pure, lovely, admirable, excellent or praiseworthy—think about such things."* Philippians 4:8 (paraphrase)

Don't get me wrong, I don't always think of these things (I wish I did), but when I catch myself going down the rabbit hole, I try really hard (and I mean it) to squint my eyes and try to picture these things. I remind myself of His promises (my future), of who He says I am (my identity), and slowly start to climb out of my negative thoughts (cave/hole).

It is my hope that this journal will give you space to focus on the good things, the beautiful things, the excellent things and that you will find, like I did, an inner peace and a better way of life.

−STEFAN KUNZ

WHATEVER

IS

Right Noble Lovely

TRUE OR PURE

THINK ON THESE

THINGS

PHILIPPIANS 4:8

DaySpring

LIVE YOUR FAITH

THE LORD IS close TO THE BROKENHEARTED & SAVES THOSE CRUSHED IN SPIRIT

·INSPIRED BY·
PSALM 34:18

DON'T FORGET TO DO GOOD

HEBREWS 13:16 NLT

INSPIRED BY I JOHN 3:18

trust in the Lord with all your Heart

PROVERBS 3:5 NLT

Seek the Kingdom of God Above All Else

MATTHEW 6:33 NLT

IF *God* IS F⇒ US ·WHO· *Could* BE against US

—INSPIRED BY—
ROMANS 8:31

the
LORD
is my
Shepherd
I shall not
want
Psalm 23:1 ESV

BE
STRONG
AND TAKE
HEART

PSALM 27:14 NIV

GOD IS OUR REFUGE AND STRENGTH AN EVER PRESENT HELP IN TROUBLE

PSALM 46:1 NIV

NEVER STOP PRAYING

1 THESSALONIANS 5:17 NLT

FAITH CAN MOVE MOUNTAINS

— INSPIRED BY MATTHEW 17:20

But SEEK First The Kingdom of God

MATTHEW 6:33 ESV

Blessed are the peacemakers for they will be called children of God

MATTHEW 5:9 NIV

LOVE
IS
PATIENT

I CORINTHIANS 13:4 NIV

LOVED YOU AT YOUR DARKEST

INSPIRED BY ROMANS 5:8

Love Endures All Things

INSPIRED BY I CORINTHIANS 13:7

Be Joyful IN HOPE PATIENT IN AFFLICTION Faithful IN Prayer

ROMANS 12:12 NIV

REJOICE — IN THE — LORD ALWAYS & AGAIN I SAY REJOICE

INSPIRED BY PHILIPPIANS 4:4

I have PLANS TO GIVE YOU Hope AND A Future

INSPIRED BY JEREMIAH 29:11

BETTER IS ONE DAY WITH YOU THAN A THOUSAND ELSEWHERE

INSPIRED BY PSALM 84:10

You're my every thing

I CORINTHIANS 15:43 ESV

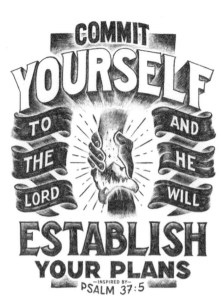

COMMIT YOURSELF TO THE LORD AND HE WILL ESTABLISH YOUR PLANS

—INSPIRED BY—
PSALM 37:5

AND death shall be no more

Revelation
21:4 ESV

Faith is the ASSURANCE of Things HOPED FOR

HEBREWS 11:1 ESV

I JOHN 4:19 ESV

In Your Presence There is Fullness of Joy

PSALM 16:11 ESV

THE HOLY Spirit HELPS US IN OUR WEAKNESS.

ROMANS 8:26 NLT

LET US RUN THE Race WITH ENDURANCE THAT —IS— SET Before US

INSPIRED BY
HEBREWS 12:1